DEEP STRENGTHS

DEEP
STRENGTHS

GETTING TO THE HEART
OF HIGH PERFORMANCE

Price Pritchett

New York   Chicago   San Francisco   Lisbon   London
Madrid   Mexico City   Milan   New Delhi   San Juan   Seoul
Singapore   Sydney   Toronto

The *McGraw·Hill* Companies

1 2 3 4 5 6 7 8 9 0   DOC/DOC 0 9 8 7

ISBN-13: 978-0-07-148546-3
ISBN-10:   0-07-148546-5

McGraw-Hill books are available at special quantity discounts to use as premiums and sales promotions, or for use in corporate training programs. For more information, please write to the Director of Special Sales, Professional Publishing, McGraw-Hill, Two Penn Plaza, New York, NY 10121-2298. Or contact your local bookstore.

Library of Congress Cataloging-in-Publication Data

Pritchett, Price.
  Deep strengths / by Price Pritchett.
     p. cm.
  Includes bibliographical references and index.
   ISBN-13: 978-0-07-148546-3 (alk. paper)
   ISBN-10: 0-07-148546-5 (alk. paper)
  1. Organizational effectiveness. 2. Personnel management. I. Title.
HD58.9.P75 2008
658.4'01--dc22
2007032972

This book is printed on acid-free paper.

Dedicated to
Early Price Pritchett, Jr.

…my dad, and an inspiration in deep strengths

CONTENTS

ACKNOWLEDGMENTS

Bringing a new book into the world takes a number of midwives. I did the writing, but Deep Strengths *was born with the help of many other people.*

Joe Aberger, president of PRITCHETT, LP, is a steadfast friend and committed leader whose dedication and talent freed me to go into seclusion, think, and put words on paper. Dr. Kim Webster played a key role in shaping and enriching the message, and Sandi Richards helped protect me from getting reckless in my writing. As usual, though, my wife Patty was the most important reader and reality check before I passed the manuscript to my publisher.

Jeanne Glasser, Editorial Director of McGraw-Hill Trade, seized on the idea of developing our Deep Strengths Research Report into a book. Jeanne, Terry Deal, Anthony Landi, Seth Morris, and the rest of the McGraw-Hill team brought great support and have been a genuine pleasure to work with.

Special thanks go to the several hundred CEOs and entrepreneurs who participated in our research project. They brought the insider-perspective on the importance of deep strengths, and I hope this book will help them build these crucial resources in their organizations.

P R I C E   P R I T C H E T T
August 2007

Preface

Houston's July heat made the shirt stick to my back as I parked my Chevy and walked into the Veterans Administration Hospital. It was Thursday, time for my one o'clock session, and I dreaded it like hell.

Nine pairs of eyes watched me enter the group therapy room. I scanned the place and saw a range of expressions: simmering anger on the face of the big guy…weariness and resignation on a couple of others…a spark of hope and energy over on the left. The air conditioner was raging and the sweat drooling down my back began to cool, so I grinned and got down to business.

I was doing an internship for my Ph.D. in psychology. Twice a week I spent an hour and a half counseling these veterans who were transitioning out of the psychiatric ward and back into the world of work. At least, that was the idea. But we were struggling.

Once again my group of guys started down the usual depressing road, sharing play-by-play accounts of how badly the world was treating them. Maybe the heat got to me on this particular day…I don't know. But after half an hour or so of their complaining and commiserating, I couldn't take it anymore, so I hit my feet and headed to the blackboard.

For the rest of the session I used chalk and lectured—about personal accountability, the power of choice, and how they could engineer positive relationships to change their lives. That impromptu rant, decades ago, was the genesis of this book. The ideas that bubbled up inside me that sweltering summer day show up here as the core concepts for developing deep strengths.

So what do I mean by the term deep strengths?

I'll get there, but let me give you a little more background. After getting the doctorate I aimed my career toward the business world, building a consulting firm that was the first in the world to specialize in merger integration strategy. Over the years we've had the opportunity to work with the best of corporate America as these companies wrestle with the challenges of major organizational change. Our job? Guide executives and their workforces through uncertainty, pain, and upheaval...bring out the best in the people...help the organizations adapt to a rapidly changing planet.

But I finally figured out that something terribly important is missing: organizations are working hard to adapt to change, but doing virtually nothing to develop deep strengths.

Why does this matter?

It matters because deep strengths are those attributes we depend on to carry us through the most difficult episodes of our lives. They're the psychological assets that also enable us to make the most of opportunity. If we want to become more effective at dealing with high-velocity change, if we wish to develop as individuals or organizations, this is where we should start.

Part One of this book explains the concept of deep strengths, presents the findings from our Deep Strengths Research Project with chief executive officers and entrepreneurs, then lays the foundation for "strength training." Part Two provides a methodology, a process for building deep strengths in individuals and organizations.

Finally, Part Three offers specific tactics for implementing strength-building practices on a day-to-day basis.

As a frustrated young intern sweating it out in a group therapy session so many years ago, I drew heavily on common sense to make my points. Today we can turn to sophisticated research for proof that these concepts and practices prepare us best for the challenges and opportunities that are sure to come.

Pillars of Organizational Effectiveness

Chapter 1

What Makes an Organization Strong?

The first organization any of us belongs to is family, so let's begin with this scenario.

BUILDING A HUMAN BEING

Imagine that you're a parent with a young family, and let's say you have a choice: You can give your four-year-old $100,000 in hard cash or you can give the child resilience. Take your pick. Which would be worth more to your offspring—big dollars, or having this personal strength to rely on in the years to come? What about staying power, the psychological strength to persevere? Would you rather bequeath that to your child, or stick another $100,000 into his or her trust fund? Next, consider attributes like confidence, hope, and a high energy level; a can-do attitude, cre-ativity, and competitive spirit; maybe ambition and happiness. At $100,000 each, would you want your child to get the money or the deep strengths?

Here's a chance to give your four-year-old a cool million. By age twenty-one, this nest egg could grow to an easy $2,500,000, and your youngster should be financially set for the future.

Problem is, the kid would be psychologically bankrupt.

Think you wouldn't sell out your son or daughter so cheaply? Okay, let's up the ante.

How about a million dollars apiece in lieu of these 10 traits? That's $10 million into your child's private account right now, probably worth $25 million by the time your child graduates from college (but the odds would turn against his or her ever finishing and getting a degree).

Which hits you as being more valuable to this young per-son—deep pockets or deep strengths? Would the fortune seem worth it if you had to watch your weak, unhappy child struggle and fail in dealing with life's everyday challenges? Would your kid find all those bucks worth the misery of being emotionally broke?

And how do you believe other people would size up the situation? Do you think they'd see all that money and take it as proof that you'd raised a strong child?

Not if they looked very close. They'd shake their heads and say, "The poor little weakling...all that money, but such a bleak future." Even the fortune itself would look fragile in the hands of a person so short on emotional assets. You'd be afraid to turn over control of the purse strings.

WHY MONEY ISN'T THE BEST MEASURING STICK

Now imagine a different situation.

Let's say you're running a business and the numbers look good. From a dollars and cents standpoint, things appear to be in fine shape. So is it a strong company?

It's worthwhile for its leaders to stop and consider where strength actually comes from.

- **Where should you look to ascertain just how robust or capable your organization actually is?**

- **What do you measure in order to determine its power?**

- **How can you best direct your efforts to make it stronger for the challenges that lie ahead?**

The common practice in assessing the strength of a business is to focus on financials, such as cash flow, income statements, the balance sheet, stock price, and so on. Certainly, these are crucial metrics, but we need to recognize the difference between cause and effect. The numbers are best seen as *effects*. Good financials are results brought about by something else.

If we really want to be results-oriented, we first should become more cause-oriented. This means looking deeper, well past the effects reflected in the financial picture, to find the hidden forces that are actually driving performance. We have to enter a forgotten region that holds the answer to the organization's best possible future.

We need to look for causes that reside in the realm of deep strengths.

THE POWER OF THE CORPORATE PSYCHE

This inner domain is where performance truly begins. It's the corporate psyche, the collective consciousness of an organization, the mental and emotional state that's at the very root of people's behavior. Now, this is not the same as the old familiar notions of morale. Or climate. Or even culture. This is different. It's the psychological dimension formed by what people are thinking and feeling, the birthplace of all that will later be defined as results. What goes on in this all-important mind space shapes what an individual does and then, collectively, how the organization as a whole ultimately performs. Results—whether they turn out to be good, bad, or ugly—are born and raised here.

This is the zone that holds the mighty influence of deep strengths, positive attributes like these:

RESILIENCE:

The ability to take problems in stride; to bounce back quickly from difficulties or defeat; change-adaptive

CONFIDENCE:

Organizational self-assurance; belief in the organization's ability to perform effectively

ENERGY LEVEL:

The "corporate metabolism"; vitality; the capacity to do work

CREATIVITY AND INNOVATION:

Coming up with viable new ideas; implementing fresh approaches

CAN-DO ATTITUDE:

A success-minded bias to "go for it" and make things happen

AMBITION:

Aspiration level or drive to achieve

HOPE:

Faith in the future; favorable outlook regarding things to come

HAPPINESS:

Positive, upbeat mental state; sense of well-being

COMPETITIVE SPIRIT:

Playing to win; determination to outdo the opposition; pushing to improve

STAYING POWER:

Emotional stamina; the psychological strength to persevere

Just think how valuable these emotional assets are to you personally. Consider the sweeping influence they have on your performance and quality of life.

Also think about the organizations you belong to. Where would they score on these important attributes? Traditionally, deep strengths don't get measured at all. It's also hard to find organizations, or for that matter, even individuals, with meaningful efforts aimed at developing themselves in this regard.

The common preoccupation is with results—with *effects*—when we should be going deeper. The secret to improvement lies in *causes*. We need to focus on the hidden drivers of performance if we want to muscle up results. The way to bring out the best in ourselves and our organizations is to develop our deep strengths.

Results are what you expect;
consequences are what you get.

— **ANONYMOUS**

Chapter 2

The Deep Strengths Research Project

I've spent three decades as an advisor to chief executive officers, their boards of directors, and other senior managers, with all of these leaders intent on building stronger, more effective outfits. Their strategies and tactics run the gamut: mergers and acquisitions, new systems and processes, product innovation, outsourcing and offshoring, training and development initiatives. The list goes on and on, but all these efforts are in search of positive change.

What we at PRITCHETT, LP wanted to know was how CEOs, in particular, look at the role deep strengths play in this process.

Our initial study gathered input from over 300 CEOs running some of the largest organizations in the United States. We surveyed 181 chief executives of for-profit enterprises, plus another 131 who preside over not-for-profits. The organizations represented in our study range in size up to 120,000 employees and $50 billion in revenue.

Even though the not-for-profits were not identified by sector, the following for-profit industries are represented in our database: Agriculture, Banking, Broadcasting, Business Services, Computer/Software, Health Care, Housing/Construction, Insurance, Manufacturing, Pharmaceuticals, Real Estate, Retail, Transportation, and Utilities.

Subsequently, PRITCHETT, LP conducted a second survey with 64 executives from small entrepreneurial companies.

HOW IMPORTANT ARE THE DEEP STRENGTHS?

One of the key questions we posed in our research was, "How much influence do you believe these 10 deep strengths have on the operating effectiveness of organizations?"

CEOs carry ultimate responsibility for operating results and their organizations' overall financial well-being. We wanted their hard-nosed, no-nonsense perspective on how deep strengths affect core performance. So the question was pointed at how their organizations operate. Our intent was to explore whether deep strengths do more than contribute merely as some kind of feel-good factor, in other words, whether they go beyond being something that's "nice to have but not essential." Since organizational strength is conventionally viewed from the financial angle, we wanted to know if CEOs think deep strengths favorably affect the bottom line.

As the chart on page 17 shows, CEOs take a clear and emphatic position: deep strengths are critically important to the success of an organization. Both for-profit and not-for-profit executives perceive virtually the same degree of "high influence" on operating effectiveness. While entrepreneurs report a little less influence, they basically share the convictions of the two CEO groups.

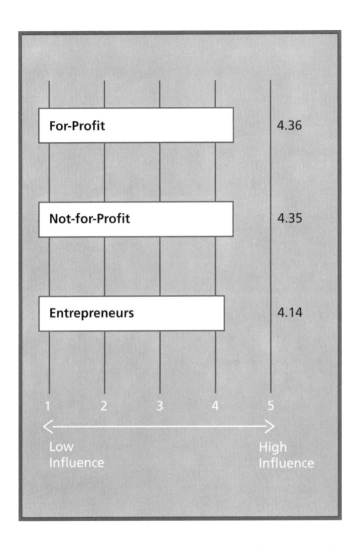

CEOs' Impression of Impact of Deep Strengths
on Their Companies' Bottom Line

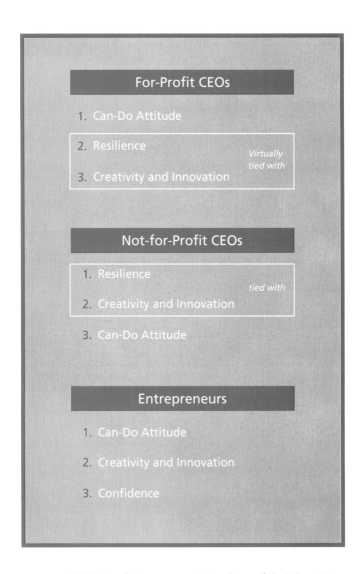

For-Profit CEOs

1. Can-Do Attitude

2. Resilience
   Virtually tied with

3. Creativity and Innovation

Not-for-Profit CEOs

1. Resilience
   tied with

2. Creativity and Innovation

3. Can-Do Attitude

Entrepreneurs

1. Can-Do Attitude

2. Creativity and Innovation

3. Confidence

CEOs' and Entrepreneurs' Ranking of the Three Deep Strengths Most Important to Their Organizations

WHICH DEEP STRENGTHS COUNT THE MOST?

It's fair to say, of course, that not all deep strengths are created equal. Some surely will influence an organization's success more than others.

We asked CEOs and entrepreneurs to "list in rank order the three deep strengths most important to your organization's success." Their rankings are shown on page 18.

As the chart shows, the "big three" are the same for both CEO groups, but with differences in their perceived order of importance. Entrepreneurs basically concur on the importance of can-do attitude and creativity and innovation, but rank confidence well above resilience in relative importance.

WHAT MATTERS LEAST?

Often it sheds light on a subject to approach it through the back door. So we encouraged these executives to consider the 10 deep strengths from a reverse angle. Specifically, we asked, "Which one of the 10 deep strengths do you consider least important for your organization's success?"

The results show that for-profit CEOs consider hope to be the least important of the 10 factors. No other deep strength comes even close. Entrepreneurs follow the same pattern, ranking hope as the least important by a very wide margin. Not-for-profit CEOs consider competitive spirit to be the least important to their organizations' success, but hope trails close behind with the second-lowest ranking.

If hope really is the least important of the deep strengths, that makes a powerful statement about how crucial all 10 of them are. Let's review some additional research that makes the point.

PSYCHOLOGICAL CAPITAL

A study of almost 4,000 college students found that fresh-men's level of hope predicted college grades more accurately than either their SAT scores or grade point averages in high school.[1] This implies that hope can have a major impact on a group's performance.

Harvard Business Review reports another study that found a strong linkage between positive emotion (for example, optimism, hope, etc.) and higher creativity, while negative emotion resulted in lower creativity. The researchers found that on days when people were in the most positive moods, they were 50 percent more likely to have creative ideas than on other days. There also was a surprising carry-over effect. The more positive someone's mood was on a given day, the more creative thinking occurred the next day and, to some extent, even the day after that. Positive emotions were found to have a simi-lar beneficial effect on productivity, commitment, and collegiality in the workplace.[2]

One of the most interesting findings in our Deep Strengths Research Project was that, while top executives consider creativity and innovation to be one of the most important deep strengths for their organizations' future success, all three groups rank their organizations the lowest on this factor. What's the most promising approach for addressing this dilemma? Rather than try to teach "techniques" for becoming more innovative, why not concentrate on developing a more positive and hopeful organizational frame of mind that is most conducive to creativity?

Paul Stoltz, author of *Adversity Quotient*, states, "Innovation is, in essence, an act of hope."[3] This suggests how the silent psychology of an organization operates, how the deep strengths are intertwined, and how they represent a new and precious class of organizational assets.

I opened up a yogurt, and underneath the lid it said, "Please try again" because they were having a contest I was unaware of. But I thought I might have opened the yogurt wrong. Or maybe Yoplait was trying to inspire me. Come on, Mitchell, don't give up, please try again! A message of inspiration from your friends at Yoplait. Fruit on bottom, Hope on top.

— MITCH HEDBERG

Chapter 3

A New Leadership Priority:
Build the Psychological Balance Sheet

Deep strengths are driven by optimism and positive relationships. The more we nudge people's thoughts and feelings in a positive direction, the more we contribute to the psychological balance sheet of the organization.

INVISIBLE ASSETS

Over the years deep strengths have grown in importance because the nature of work has dramatically changed. It's probably safe to say that today's knowledge work is 90 percent cognitive, that is, mental and emotional, while a mere 10 percent is physical.

- **The *mind* is now the main productivity tool.**

- ***Thinking* has become the key competence.**

- **People's *thought processes* are the major source of wealth creation.**

"What's going on in people's heads" deserves serious attention because the organization's key assets reside inside the skulls of its workforce.

Since job performance now depends so heavily on cognitive effectiveness, leadership is becoming far more psychological in nature. The new challenge is to become adroit at managing the corporate psyche in a positive direction. This collective consciousness or group mind is the very bedrock of behavior, governing the total organization and its interactions with the environment. What your organization thinks, feels, and says to itself will determine its day-to-day performance, its win-loss record that shows up in the annual report, its very destiny.

THE COST OF UNHAPPINESS

Some executives might question whether happiness deserves to be considered a deep strength. The easiest way to answer this is to look at the costs associated with a negative corporate psyche.

Even if happiness doesn't help drive your organization's top line, a lack of it certainly can damage its bottom line. Happiness is essentially the opposite of depression, which the World Health Organization (WHO) recently declared to be the world's fourth most debilitating condition, behind heart disease, cancer, and traffic accidents. WHO also predicts that depression will become the *second* most debilitating condition worldwide by 2020. *US News & World Report* states, "People today are 10 times as likely to suffer from depression as those born two generations ago."[4] *The Wall Street Journal* reports, "According to the National Institute of Mental Health in Bethesda, MD, 9.5 percent of U.S. adults suffer from depression."[5] You might take a minute and run this calculation on *your* organization:

$$9.5\% \times \underline{\hspace{3cm}} = \underline{\hspace{4cm}}$$

your employee population   *number of clinically depressed people potentially on your payroll*

A shortage of happiness probably adds substantially to the health care costs in your organization.

Beyond being a financial drain from a medical angle, though, negativity is terribly expensive in terms of how it damages employee engagement and productivity. Gallup research shows that 17 percent of all U.S. workers age 18 and older—some 22.5 million employees—are "actively disengaged." Their reduced productivity reportedly costs the U.S. economy about $300 billion a year.[6]

THE MAGIC RATIO OF 5 TO 1

Nevertheless, crusty managers and other skeptics are leery of being positive. They worry that others might take advantage of the situation or become too complacent. What's ironic, though, is how difficult it is to find people who say they *personally* respond best to negative rather than positive treatment. In fact, 99 percent of people polled say they would prefer a more positive work environment.[7]

A long-running research program with implications for management has been conducted by a psychologist named John Gottman. His research involved hundreds of couples who had just received their marriage licenses. While each couple interacted for 15 minutes, observers counted the number of positive versus negative exchanges between the two people. Then the researchers predicted who would divorce. Decades-long follow-up studies produced stunning results, revealing that the researchers had achieved 94 percent accuracy in predicting which marriages would fail. The basis for the initial forecasts was that couples who had fewer than five positive interactions for each negative interaction would be at risk for splitting up, and the projections proved amazingly accurate.[8]

Since then similar studies have been conducted in the work environment with comparable results. Groups with a positive to negative interaction ratio of at least 3 to 1 are more productive than teams with lower ratios. The so-called magic ratio, however, is 5 to 1—five positive interactions for every negative interaction. This combination appears to bring out an organization's best performance.

Can a person be too positive? Probably so. The upper limit seems to be 13 to 1, with evidence suggesting that things are likely to worsen when work groups exceed that ratio. Still, the challenge for practically all organizations is to become more positive, not less, because that's how you build the psychological balance sheet.

I think my new thing will be to try to be a real happy guy. I'll just walk around being real happy until some jerk says something stupid to me.

— JACK HANDEY

Chapter 4

What Should "Strength Training" Look Like?

Deep strengths are deemed highly important by many of the country's leaders, but how can individuals and organizations muscle up? What's the most direct approach to developing these psychological assets? Instead of hoping it will happen by chance, let's consider how you can deliberately create a strengths-building culture.

THE POWER OF OTHER PEOPLE

It's tough to build deep strengths in isolation. To a large extent, these attributes are shaped through human connections...through the ordinary social give-and-take that we have with other people. We all move through the hours, days, and years interpreting our stream of person-to-person experiences in ways that either develop or diminish our deep strengths.

Close relationships may carry the most punch, but even casual encounters leave their mark on our psychological makeup. Each interaction brings new data that we may use to make inferences about our abilities. Every social exchange represents one more chance to draw conclusions about who we are, our worth as a human being, and how we'll approach the situation at hand.

Ordinarily this mental processing occurs automatically. We quietly, relentlessly, and, for the most part, unconsciously do our sense-making of everyday life. Positive, uplifting episodes help us feel better about ourselves and help our deep strengths flourish. Negative experiences cause the deep strengths to decay.

Here's the problem: too much of the time people just "do what comes naturally" in dealing with one another. They let nature take its course, rather than consciously and deliberately managing social exchanges in a positive direction. As a result, most of their encounters contribute nothing to the enhancement of deep strengths, and far too many actually do damage.

WORK:
A LABORATORY FOR BUILDING DEEP STRENGTHS

Organizations provide an excellent practice field for strength training because they're based on structured human contact. We just need to act purposefully, follow a practical regimen, and be determined to grow in this regard.

Leaders should, as the label implies, take the lead.

Deep strengths represent a new and powerful leverage point for those who seek to position their organizations for excellence in the years to come. CEOs, Chief Learning Officers, and leaders in general carry prime responsibility for putting deep strengths on the organizational dash-board, where they are looked at, talked about, measured, and developed.

The better we get at engineering positive exchanges with others, the more we develop deep strengths and can look forward to a better future, both individually and collectively. However we go as individuals, so go our organizations.

THE POWER OF REPETITION

Of course, we need to respect the fact that strength training, whether physical or psychological, takes time. Building deep strengths requires a sustained effort, much like what's involved in building a muscular, well-defined physique.

For example, nobody thinks in terms of developing strong biceps by lifting 15,000 pounds all at once, just one time. Instead, you lift maybe 50 pounds...for 10 repetitions...three times a week...for 10 weeks. Same total amount of weight lifted—15,000 pounds—but according to a regimen that builds muscle and increases your strength rather than breaking your back.

You schedule your workouts to give your body the time it needs to grow. And you keep at it.

If you have that kind of commitment, all you need is technique. So now let's focus on the person-to-person methodology for developing deep strengths.

Strength does not come from physical capacity. It comes from an indomitable will.

— **M A H A T M A   G A N D H I**

The Person-to-Person High-Performance Model

Chapter 5

The Heart of the Matter:
Action-Reaction Behavior Cycles

What do you have planned for today?

It's a pretty sure bet that you'll be dealing with other human beings. It could be your boss or somebody who works for you. It might be a person you're serving in some capacity, or a random individual out on the street. It may be a friend or family member. In fact, chances are you'll have contact with one person after another until you call it quits tonight and fall asleep.

I don't know who you'll run into today, but *I can tell you what's going to happen.*

Not everything—just enough to give you incredible influence over how those people treat you, how they feel about themselves, and how well all of you perform.

PREDICTING THE FUTURE

Some human behavior can be predicted with amazing accuracy, and that's what this book will reveal. With that particular knowledge and insight, you'll be able in most instances to evoke the behaviors and attitudes you want from others. This holds true whether you want people to be pleasant, helpful, and upbeat...whether you wish to pick a fight or want to make someone feel worse...or whether you prefer that other folks simply leave you alone. You can engineer situations in the direction you choose. But you will choose. So you need to be aware of what you're doing. You also need to know how the social dynamics always work and be willing to live with the ramifications of your decisions.

Most people fail to realize how predictable human beings actually are. Likewise, most of us are unaware of how much we personally shape other people's emotions and behavior. To be truthful about it, we really don't like the idea that misbehavior, meanness, or poor performance on the part of others could be happening because of us. That would put us in the inconvenient position of needing to change ourselves. But like it or not, each of us is a force in the lives of those around us. We have an effect on the people we encounter, and each of us is accountable for whether our presence proves to be for better or for worse. Even when we're not to blame for other people's shortcomings, we can produce big improvements in them by maintaining positive behavior in our half of the relationship.

Why go to the trouble? Because the old saying is true: "What goes around comes around." Being a positive influence on others contributes to our own effectiveness and well-being. If you make an effort to build other people's deep strengths, you're bound to develop your own.

We all live in reciprocal relationships—social exchanges—or what you might think of as person-to-person loops. This means we cannot escape our own sphere of influence. The effect we have on the people we encounter generally boomerangs back in our direction. We're still within range ourselves, still susceptible to others' reactions to our behavior, such that whatever influence we transmit will typically soon come home to roost.

SMALL MOMENTS

The exchanges we have with other people often seem complex and hard to manage. So let's take an approach that simplifies relationships and makes them easy to understand.

Life comes at us in small bits—tiny episodes—little stitches of time that register in our minds and become the fabric of our being. According to Nobel Prize–winner Dr. Daniel Kahneman, we experience about 20,000 of these individual moments in each working day. They last about three seconds each. The most memorable moments are almost always positive or negative, not neutral.

These mini-experiences include the brief social exchanges that serve as the basic building blocks of your interpersonal relationships. If you understand what happens at the person-to-person level in these small moments, all of a sudden you're able to predict key aspects of what's coming as you deal with the people around you. Knowing how to operate socially in these fleeting episodes also presents a remarkable opportunity to influence events in a constructive direction.

The fact is, you can identify clear patterns in the small moments you share with another person. The patterns are wonderfully simple. They're so easy to read. And they are always present.

You just have to pay attention, plus form the habit of consciously managing your part of the back-and-forth between yourself and others. Once you learn what to look for, then embrace a couple of key principles, you're in business. And it's going to make a striking difference in your life.

ACTION-REACTION BEHAVIOR CYCLES

There are distinct roles and a natural rhythm in one-on-one encounters. Regardless of who the two people are, and no matter what the circumstances, you're probably going to observe the same scenario. It plays out like this: one person acts, and the other reacts. The cycle is complete...the relationship is off and running. Pretty straightforward.

Let's stop here for a minute. The little model on page 49—the Action-Reaction Behavior Cycle—will help you analyze the nature of relationships and why they develop the way they do. It's sort of like a social road map that shows how the behavior traffic runs between two people. The Action-Reaction Behavior Cycle reveals who's doing what in one of life's small moments. It's a simple diagram, but it captures the essence of the exchange and gives a penetrating diagnosis of how smart we're being in our behavior.

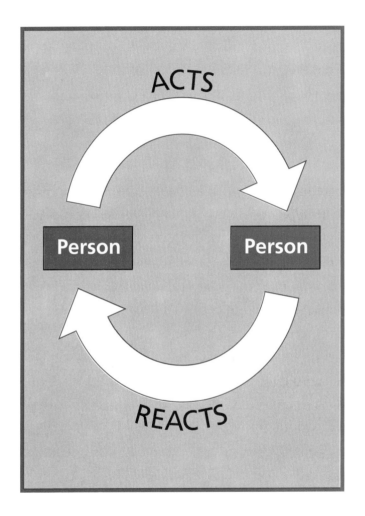

Action-Reaction Behavior Cycle

If you chart where you are in a cycle with another person (acting or reacting), and then note how both of you are behaving (nice, mean, or neither), you'll find it instructive. This quick little analysis also helps you decide how to maneuver. Obviously, some moves will serve you far better than others, and it may surprise you to discover which are the most promising.

Just remember—life is a social affair. We live in a world of human give-and-take. And whatever behaviors we decide to give out toward others will heavily influence what we find ourselves obliged to take in return.

❚❚ *I make mistakes.*
　　　I'll be the second to admit it. **❚❚**

　　　　　　— J E A N　　K E R R

Chapter 6

Your Hot-Wired Emotional Brain

Picture this situation: You've just finished lunch and are headed back to work. Walking along, you come face-to-face with another person. You're six feet apart and closing. Eye contact! Then...

This is such an ordinary sort of encounter—just one of your day's 20,000 small moments. We breeze through many of these episodes without even thinking, or so we believe. But in fact there's a decision-making process beginning inside your head, and it confronts you with a couple of choices.

But wait!

Before you have time to decide *anything*, a fascinating exchange takes place between you and the other person. It's invisible. But functional magnetic resonance imaging (fMRI) machines can pick it up on neural scans as they track the electrical activity in your two brains. A two-person circuitry develops, a remote brain-to-brain connection, locking you together in a neural link that operates beneath your awareness. This person-to-person feedback loop occurs at a blazing speed, faster even than your ability to think. And it's involuntary. You're engaged with one another instantly, like it or not.

EMOTIONAL SPEED-READING:
THE INFLUENCE OF MIRROR NEURONS

Research with neuroimaging techniques reveals that we're actually wired to behave before we think. At the same time as your brain's centers for thought are just gearing up to deal with a social encounter, but too soon for you to consciously analyze the situation at hand, other parts of the brain move at hyperspeed to deal with the circumstances. Mirror neurons—your brain cells for social reconnaissance—start firing away. Their job has three parts: sense what the other person is about to do, tune in to that person's feelings, then prepare you to imitate that person's movement and be empathetic. All this happens subliminally, outside the reach of your conscious awareness.

The mirror neurons go flat out, making their hair-trigger emotional assessment and priming you for matching behavior. Like a sixth sense, they operate in a purely spontaneous manner. You're not in charge of this activity at all. It's as automatic as your heartbeat.

Before you can consciously figure out how you want to behave, much less have enough time to actually do whatever you might decide, signals from the other person begin shaping your behavior. Your mirror neurons do their detective work and, in a flash, prompt you to move in a parallel manner. You can't help yourself. The "mirroring" is a reflecting back of the behavior you observe in someone else. Feelings you unconsciously perceive in the other individual are instantly sensed inside, and your natural reflex is to mimic that person's emotional state.

Naturally, this mirroring process is a two-way street. You're always revealing yourself to other people's mirror neurons, sending out your own signals which immediately influence how they feel and behave. This happens whether you're connecting face-to-face, voice-to-voice, or skin-to-skin. It doesn't matter whether you're trying to come across a certain way, or if you're oblivious to the signals you're sending. You're under surveillance. Their mirror neurons size you up in milliseconds, then mimic you or at least create the impulse to do so. The result? Your feelings aren't felt by you alone, but also by anybody within range. This helps explain why emotions are so contagious.

THE SECRET TO MANAGING FIRST IMPRESSIONS

Your first crack at influencing others, then, occurs in the initial 1/20th of a second of your encounter! That's a mighty small window of opportunity. You can't think that fast. So if you want to influence others to behave a certain way, you need to already *be that way* when their mirror neurons fire off in your direction. Whatever emotion or behavior you want mirrored back toward you must already be in place, waiting within you, ready for other people to read it.

The good news is that other people can't avoid the impulse to behave like you. The bad news? Well, if you make a first impression that's negative, you literally program them to be negative too. They may fight the urge to match your mood and manner, but the natural inclination will be to reciprocate. Their mirror neurons' job is to synchronize with you emotionally.

Most of the signals people focus on will come from your face, particularly your eyes, in fleeting micro-expressions. They'll also pick up signals from your tone of voice, gestures, and body language in general. But what you say—the actual words you use—will count for nothing in this instant assessment process. Mirror neurons believe in what they can sense rather than what you might have to say.

Just how sensitive are the mirror neurons? Studies show they can be triggered merely by looking at pictures of other people. For example, Swedish researchers found that they could activate muscles involved in the smiling response just by showing people photographs of happy faces. As Harvard psychologist Dr. Daniel Goleman writes in *Social Intelligence*,

"Indeed, whenever we gaze at a photograph of someone whose face displays a strong emotion, like sadness, disgust, or joy, our facial muscles automatically start to mirror the other's facial expression."[9]

WHY THE CONSCIOUS MIND IS NEEDED

Mirroring is a cornerstone of our social skills. It helps us read people and get on the same emotional wavelength. Mirror neurons put us in synch with others, cue up empathic responses, and prompt the urge to act. They also create the very first person-to-person loop. This unconscious connection serves as the launch pad for a relationship, the staging ground for Action-Reaction Behavior Cycles that may follow.

Problem is, your emotion-driven mirroring impulses can also work to your disadvantage. Sometimes these neurons misread the other person or leap to a wrong conclusion. Other times they size up the situation accurately, but you're better off not doing what comes naturally. That's when you need help from the prefrontal cortex, the thinking part of your brain.

Even if your mirror neurons are serving you beautifully, they aren't equipped to handle your social interactions all by themselves. They're just your scout team. You'll need immediate reinforcements—specifically, conscious thought—to help you navigate the two decision points that are rapidly closing in on you.

So now let's pick up where we left off at the beginning of this chapter.

Lunch is over and you're hurrying back to work. Rounding a corner, oops! You're maybe two steps away from someone. Eyes lock. Mirror neurons fire back and forth. Then your thinking brain kicks into gear and starts wrestling with a couple of slippery choices that demand immediate attention.

A loving person lives in a loving world.
A hostile person lives in a hostile world:
Everyone you meet is your mirror.

— **KEN KEYES, JR.**

Chapter 7

The Edge

Imagine the mini-drama that unfolds when you encounter another person.

If we catch this event on camera, or simply watch from a distance, we'll see a new person-to-person loop take shape. This one follows immediately after the mirror neuron exchange that fired between the two of you. But this new loop has thought behind it. Conscious intent.

Opening scene: In a flash, your thinking brain sizes up the social landscape, charts your course, and sends you into an Action-Reaction Behavior Cycle. This cycle develops out of two simple decisions facing you and the other person. But these decisions are so routine, and the time frame for deciding is so tight, that people overlook the fact that they're making conscious choices.

The social drama in these small moments is rich even though your choices are limited.

DECISION 1:
DO I WANT TO ACT OR REACT?

Your first decision point offers an either-or choice. You need to decide which part of the Behavior Cycle you want to occupy. Would you prefer to be the person who initiates action, or the one who plays the reaction role?

Act or react—what difference does it make anyhow?

Well, it could make all the difference in how the situation unfolds. Whoever seizes the initiative gains a degree of social advantage. Make the opening move, and you create psychological pressure for a matching reaction. It's your chance to influence how people treat you, your opportunity to shape their behavior and attitude in a good direction. Sure, they may resist the urge, but they will feel a subtle obligation to reciprocate.

Of course, if you fool around too long trying to make up your mind, other people may take this choice away from you. They're going through the same decision-making process and can preempt you by acting first. In that case, your only option is to react. *And you lose the edge.*

So why would you ever deliberately pick the reaction part of the Action-Reaction Behavior Cycle? The logic typically goes like this: "I'm going to play it safe. Seems to me that reacting is less risky. If I wait and see what the other person does, then I'll know how I want to respond." But this line of reasoning actually puts you at far greater risk. You're sacrificing influence, leaving the situation up for grabs, and forfeiting your chance to start the relationship off in the direction you choose.

Granted, now and then you'll find yourself in a sensitive situation where it makes sense to let others make the first move. Tact and good judgment may say to you, "Give the other person some space. Let the situation develop further, so you can make sure you behave appropriately." Just remember, when you allow others to own the action part of the behavior cycle, you'll be under their influence as you react.

So form the habit of deciding fast and choosing to act. Make the opening move and you gain the edge, which brings you to the next decision.

DECISION 2:
DO I WANT TO BE POSITIVE, NEGATIVE,
OR NEUTRAL?

This second decision is a bullet you can't dodge. Regardless of whether you end up in the action or reaction part of the cycle, you're forced to choose how you'll behave. So what will it be? Positive, negative, or neutral? You're free to select the emotional tone for your behavior, but you only have three options. That's it.

Nobody else can make this decision for you. Your prefrontal cortex makes the call.

At this stage of the encounter your mirror neurons have already scanned the other person and unconsciously primed you to behave a certain way. But now you get to decide whether to go with that impulse or resist the urge. Also, if the other person seized the initiative and acted first, you'll feel psychological pressure to reciprocate. Nevertheless, how you react is your choice.

Your thinking brain works slower than your mirror neurons, but it carries more clout and operates under your voluntary control. It can veto an impulse to retaliate. It can choose to remain positive when others are negative or neutral.

While your thinking brain has the final say in how you handle yourself, other people have the privilege of labeling your behavior as positive, negative, or neutral. Let's go over that again. Whoever is on the receiving end gets to classify your behavior. If you say you're smiling, and the other person in the cycle perceives it to be a sarcastic smirk, that person's opinion prevails. He or she can legitimately say you're being negative. Is this fair? Well, it holds you accountable for how you're coming across to others. And look at it this way: you will insist on the right to label the attitudes and behavior that other people aim in your direction.

THE TWO GROUND RULES FOR DEVELOPING DEEP STRENGTHS

Your two simple decisions will immediately slot you into one of six behavior categories. These are the only alternatives available to you and the other person:

- **Act positive**
- **Act negative**
- **Act neutral**
- **React positive**
- **React negative**
- **React neutral**

As you both work through your choices, a new person-to-person loop takes shape. One of you seizes the initiative and acts, the other person reacts, and each of you chooses whether to be positive, negative, or neutral. These simple decisions produce an Action-Reaction Behavior Cycle, a complete social exchange.

What will it look like?

This may surprise you: *There are only nine different Action-Reaction Behavior Cycles.* All the social drama of our relationships plays out in this limited set of person-to-person loops. We shift in and out of them constantly, flowing from one cycle into another, depending on how we handle our two simple decision points.

Just remember the two ground rules:

- **Take the initiative**
- **Be positive**

Acting first gives you the edge. Being positive develops deep strengths.

▎▎ *What is not possible*
is not to choose. **▎▎**

— **J E A N - P A U L   S A R T R E**

Chapter 8

Nine Cycles and No More

Face-to-face with another person...

You deal with the two decisions. You end up in one of six behavior categories. And depending on what the other person decides, the two of you will pair up in one of these nine Action-Reaction Behavior Cycles.

These person-to-person loops show the full range of possibilities for your interactions with other people. In the course of a routine week, you'll probably spend time in all nine cycles. The cycles are illustrated on page 74.

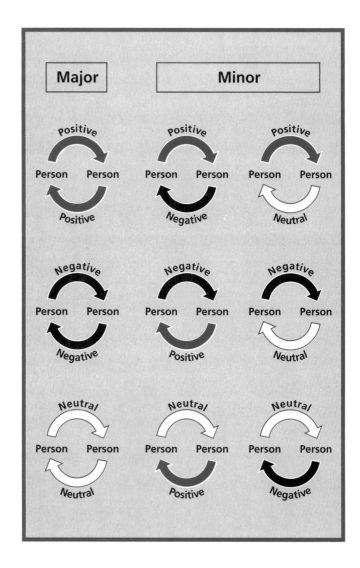

Nine Action-Reaction Cycles

THE THREE MAJOR CYCLES

People being the way they are, odds favor the development of a loop with matching emotions in both halves of the cycle. The action resembles the reaction, whether positive, negative, or neutral. This reciprocal exchange implies a tacit agreement between two people regarding how they'll relate. The matching emotions create a self-reinforcing cycle where the behavior tends to perpetuate itself.

Consider the implications. If you take the initiative and act positive, most of the time you'll elicit a positive reaction. I've polled many groups of people over the years, and they consistently say that a positive action will trigger a positive response 85 to 87 percent of the time. These are terrific odds, certainly worth your taking the risk involved in making the opening move.

The predictability shoots even higher, though, if you begin the cycle in a negative way. The likelihood of a negative reaction jumps to 90 to 95 percent, almost guaranteeing you the ability to create an unpleasant cycle at your whim.

As we know from research, negative emotions carry more impact than positive emotions.

And what about so-called neutral behavior? Again you can play the percentages. If you want people to leave you alone, or if you want emotional distance from others, go neutral. Most of the world will accommodate you.

You see a lot of neutral behavior in the matter-of-fact conversations and transactions between people, where it can be fairly useful. It also shows up in the neutral inter-actions that we'll call "elevator behavior." These are the everyday encounters where people make no emotional investment in the episode and don't even acknowledge one another. Though fully aware of each other's presence, they pass like ships in the night. You can't even determine who's acting versus who's reacting.

Here's the problem. Neutral behavior is so ambiguous, so emotionally vague, it can easily be misconstrued. Behavior that you intend to be neutral often gets labeled negative by people on the receiving end.

THE SIX MINOR CYCLES

The defining feature of minor cycles is the unfair exchange that takes place between the two people involved. One person is giving better treatment than the other. This creates an unbalanced relationship, and the big question is, "Who will prevail?"

All of us know what it feels like to be in a person-to-person loop where we're being shortchanged. It's unpleasant. Our natural impulse is to get even or get away from the other person.

So minor cycles tend to be short-lived. Without reciprocity to help them endure, they ordinarily migrate toward one of the major cycles. The two people soon resolve the imbalance in the social exchange either by parting ways or by shifting to a major cycle where they're treating one another the same.

Your thinking brain manages your behavior here.

Let's say you make the opening move with a smile and warm greeting, but the other person chooses to respond in a neutral manner. Instantly your prefrontal cortex analyzes the exchange and decides whether to label the reaction as neutral, negative, or even positive. That's your privilege, because only you know how it felt to be on the receiving end. Then the thinking brain decides what your next move will be. You can hold your ground and remain positive, maybe shift to neutral, or even make a negative move.

The six minor cycles reflect a battle of wills, a struggle between two people to control the emotional tone of the exchange. Just remember: you're always accountable for your behavior. Sure, other people may influence you, and your mirror neurons might prime you to behave a certain way, but your prefrontal cortex bats last. It can override these forces. Ultimately, you choose whether to be positive, negative, or neutral.

THE PERSON-TO-PERSON LOOP OF CHOICE

With only nine cycles to choose from, you can easily target the one that confers the most benefits. Just ask yourself three simple questions:

- **Would I prefer to live in a positive frame of mind?**

- **How do I want people to treat me?**

- **What kind of influence do I wish to have on others?**

If you want to feel positive, behave that way and the feelings will follow. If you want people to treat you in a positive manner, give their mirror neurons positive signals and initiate positive cycles. If you want to have a beneficial effect on others, send positive behavior in their direction.

Simply play the odds. They're stacked heavily in your favor.

Of course, we all slip into bad cycles now and then. Sometimes it's our own fault, sometimes we're just dealing with a difficult person. But ordinarily we can exit a bad cycle. We can break the loop of unpleasantness. Part Three describes six "power moves" that will help us build positive loops.

II *I haven't got the slightest idea how*
to change people, but still I keep a
long list of prospective candidates just
in case I should ever figure it out. *II*

— DAVID SEDARIS

Power Moves
for Strength Training

Chapter 9

The Power of Demeanor

POWER MOVE 1:
BE POSITIVE WITH YOUR BODY,
BECAUSE IT ALWAYS SPEAKS FIRST.

Your demeanor sends the first messages to the people you encounter, revealing your emotions via body language. Their mirror neurons pick up signals from your carriage, gestures, and, in particular, facial expressions. Demeanor reveals your feelings and prompts others to reciprocate, so you need to manage it every bit as carefully as you do your choice of words.

Most people presume their feelings are communicated mainly by the things they say, but most of the time our emotions are expressed through nonverbal cues. In his book, *A Whole New Mind*, Daniel Pink explains:

"Since emotion is conveyed nonverbally, to enter another's heart, you must begin the journey by looking into the face."[10]

The brain's wiring routes all of your feelings—everything from minor moods to overwhelming emotions—directly to the face. These emotions are instantly displayed, automatically and unconsciously, through the movements of close to 200 facial muscles. You can make a conscious effort to conceal or suppress how you feel, but seldom will you pull this off successfully.

The muscles that surround our eyes are especially designed to express the subtleties of emotions. This highlights the importance of eye contact, and helps explain why in social encounters our instinctive first glance is into the eyes of the other person.

The second most expressive area of the face is the mouth. In fact, the smile is the most contagious of all emotional signals. This holds true worldwide, across all cultures and age groups. Wearing a smile will serve you well, because the human brain responds most favorably to happy faces. It recognizes them better and faster than faces wearing negative expressions.

Smiling does more than predispose others to smile back at you. It also moves your emotions in a positive direction. In fact, all emotions work this way. If you intentionally set your facial muscles into a frown, you'll trigger negative feelings inside. If you put an expression of panic on your face, it will stimulate a sense of fear. Merely by changing your expression, you can create noticeable changes in the autonomic nervous system. As Malcolm Gladwell states in *Blink*, "Emotion can start on the face."[11]

This drives home the importance of deliberately managing your demeanor. Simply act "as if" you feel positive, and it will nudge you in that direction. You don't have to wait until you get lucky or just happen to feel good, you can purposefully choose the body language that will lead you there. In the process, you'll take others along with you.

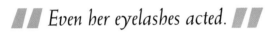 *Even her eyelashes acted.*

— VIRGINIA WOOLF

Chapter 10

The Power of Positive Expectations

POWER MOVE 2:
USE POSITIVE EXPECTATIONS TO PREDICT
THE FUTURE.

Let's make it very clear: being positive doesn't make you a pushover. It doesn't mean being soft and sacrificing results in an attempt to keep people happy. In fact, you develop deep strengths in others by doing just the opposite, that is, by expecting more of them.

The key ingredient in positive expectations is the emotional tone you express toward the other person. Merely being demanding doesn't work. But if you create a positive connection, you can hold someone to a higher standard. The bond lets you be more exacting and less tolerant of mediocrity.

How does this work?

First, your positive stance makes the other person more willing to try. Second, high expectations send a positive message implying that the person has the ability to deliver. You affirm the individual. This inspires hope, builds confidence, and brings more potential into play. Your high expectations fuel greater effort and nurture a can-do spirit.

Research proves that expectations create a self-fulfilling prophecy. A classic study by Harvard psychologist Robert Rosenthal and Lenore Jacobson involved IQ testing of students in a San Francisco elementary school.[12] The researchers told the teachers that some students had scored very high on the test and would "bloom" academically. The so-called high IQ students were actually picked at random, but the teachers were not aware of this. Teachers for the other student group, operating without this false information, presumed that their students were just normal. Follow-up IQ testing eight months later revealed that the "bloomers" had, in fact, blossomed. The mean IQ of the supposed gifted group was significantly higher than that of the "normal" group. This pattern of results, known as the "Rosenthal effect", has been found repeatedly through research in schools and other organizations.

In fact, Rosenthal and Fode produced similar results in research they conducted with animals.[13] The students were told they would be doing experiments with a new strain of super-intelligent rats that could run mazes quickly. Rosenthal then gave everyone perfectly normal rats. Half the students were told they had the new "maze-bright" animals, while the other half believed they were working with "maze-dull" rats. Students working with the so-called bright rats noticed daily improvements in maze running, with their animals running the maze faster and more accurately than the other group. Students who thought they were working with dull rats found that their animals refused to budge from the starting line 29 percent of the time, while the supposedly bright rats refused only 11 percent of the time.

Whether we intend to or not, we somehow communicate our expectations via subtle cues in our behavior. People pick up these cues, often subconsciously, and adjust their behavior to match them. The effect may be positive or negative, beneficial or detrimental, but our expectations have a habit of coming true.

You can take advantage of this self-fulfilling prophecy. Use the power of positive expectations to predict the future.

■■ The Ancient Greeks," I say, "...listened to the wind and predicted the future from that." DeWeese squints. "How could they tell the future from the wind?" "I don't know, maybe the same way a painter can tell the future of his painting by staring at the canvas. ■■

— ROBERT M. PIRSIG

Zen and the Art of Motorcycle Maintenance

Chapter 11

The Power of Positive Attention

POWER MOVE 3:

MAKE SURE OTHER PEOPLE FEEL APPRECIATED.

Positive attention offers some of the best ways to kick off positive behavior cycles and keep them going. And you don't have to utter a word.

You can convey positive attention nonverbally through eye contact, smiles, or a simple nod. Maybe you just lean in and really listen to the other person. You might use the power of touch, such as a hug, handshake, or pat on the back. It may be nothing more than a friendly wave, or giving another individual some of your time. All of it works.

People don't have to hear you say anything to get a positive message from you.

Of course, words do matter. A recent study involving 800 high-level executives found they use positive words *four* times as often as negative words.[14] But you don't have to be eloquent. You can express positive attention in very common, everyday language.

For example, we all warm to the compliments that come our way, or to a word of thanks from someone else. We feel a positive uptick in our emotions when a person asks our opinion, or when we receive words of encouragement and appreciation. Even something as mundane as hearing another person call us by name can give us a good feeling.

Do you think these behaviors are too trivial to count for much?

According to the U.S. Department of Labor, the number one reason people quit their jobs is because they don't feel appreciated. And a poll conducted by the Gallup organization found that 65 percent of people say they receive no workplace recognition in a given year.[15] If basically two out of three people are missing out on this kind of positive attention, you know it represents a perfect opportunity to improve performance.

Research proves that it pays to "catch people doing something right." People who receive regular recognition and praise become more productive. The positive attention also enhances their engagement with colleagues and reduces accidents on the job. Employees who are treated positively relay that same feeling to others, generating higher loyalty and satisfaction scores from customers. Finally, positive attention builds job commitment and reduces costly turnover.

If that's not enough to justify the effort, do it for your own selfish reasons. Giving positive attention to others may benefit you more than it does them.

What's the payoff? First, it puts you in a positive frame of mind, and that's where you need to be. Also, you'll probably elicit an appreciative response. People will reciprocate, aiming more positive attention in your direction, and that helps develop your own deep strengths.

■■ *Never call anybody an asshole.*
It hardly ever works. ■■

— **M A R I L Y N   P E T E R S O N**

Chapter 12

The Power of Positive Guiding Questions

POWER MOVE 4:

ASK QUESTIONS THAT FOCUS PEOPLE ON STRENGTHS AND SOLUTIONS.

Naguib Mahfouz, Egyptian novelist and Nobel laureate, said, "You can tell whether a man is clever by his answers. You can tell whether a man is wise by his questions."

Questions are fateful; they set the course for our conversations. Simply asking people something aims their thoughts and feelings a certain way. The wisdom lies in using questions that point people's minds in a positive direction.

Let's say someone approaches you seeking help. You can aim the dialogue toward problem talk or solution talk. For example, you could ask, "What's the problem?" Or you could start the discussion down a quite different path if you say, "What solution are you trying to achieve?" If you inquire "What's wrong?" the conversation veers toward bad things. But asking, "What results are you looking for?" orients the exchange toward positive outcomes.

Problem talk focuses on weaknesses, constraints, and breakdowns. Solution talk orients the mind toward strengths, resources, possibilities, and a successful future. Either way of talking amplifies the issues being addressed.

If you use negatively oriented questions, the dialogue will drain energy and be depressing. In contrast, positive guiding questions get people engaged and committed in the construction of action plans. The conversation energizes and inspires.

You're free to open a conversation any way you wish. It's your choice. But what you talk about and how you talk about it make a difference. You can concentrate on what's working or not working, what has been done right or where things went wrong. Either way, you immediately structure the other person's way of looking at the situation. It may not seem like a big deal. After all, it's such a simple shift in phrasing. But your approach profoundly affects the entire tone and direction of the exchange.

Questions give you a small moment of influence. They let you direct others' thoughts by focusing their attention and having them look through a mental frame of your choosing. Positive guiding questions seduce people to look at life through a favorable lens. You can use these questions as powerful levers for moving others into a positive mindset.

Just remember: whatever you focus on expands. The more you employ a positive slant in your questions, the more you improve your chances for pulling people into positive cycles.

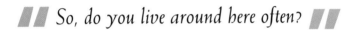 *So, do you live around here often?*

— S T E V E N   W R I G H T

Chapter 13

The Power of Funny

POWER MOVE 5:

SHOW AN EASY SENSE OF HUMOR.

Humor can be your most powerful technique for shifting people into positive behavior cycles. Laughter is one of the most direct ways to make a positive brain-to-brain connection. Dr. Daniel Goleman explains, "Laughing represents the shortest distance between two people because it instantly interlocks limbic systems."[16]

Lightheartedness, laughter, and a playful spirit activate the right side of the brain. This zone lights up when we're experiencing good feelings; when we're happy, optimistic, and positive toward others.

The therapeutic benefits of humor also extend into the realm of physical health. Laughter decreases harmful stress hormones and boosts the immune system. It brings aerobic benefits to the body and even carries analgesic properties, which means that humor truly is a painkiller!

The advantages of humor are particularly evident in our professional lives. In a recent *Harvard Business Review* article, Fabio Sala writes:

"More than four decades of study by various researchers confirm some common-sense wisdom: Humor, used skillfully, greases the management wheels. It reduces hostility, deflects criticism, relieves tension, improves morale, and helps communicate difficult messages."[17]

Studies show that the most effective leaders get people laughing two to three times more often than average executives do. These leaders who are most skilled at displaying humor rank in the top one-third of bonuses, and are rated "excellent" by 90 percent of their peers and bosses.[18]

While the latest research is showing that traditional IQ accounts for only 4 to 10 percent of career success,[19] the social intelligence trait of humor keeps going up in importance.

You might be thinking, "That's not good news. I don't have an ounce of comedian in me. I can't even tell a decent joke." Don't worry. Most of the time humor comes out of friendly banter, amusing observations about the situation at hand, or maybe from poking a little fun at oneself.

Just do something that lightens up the conversation, whatever might bring a chuckle from others. Laughter is actually more contagious than yawning, so people will most likely pitch in and help.

"" Be straightforward in
　　　the way you dodge issues. **""**

— ANONYMOUS

Chapter 14

The Power of Playing to the Sweet Spot

POWER MOVE 6:

ENGAGE PEOPLE'S UNIQUE GIFTS.

Give people a chance to play in their sweet spot, and you give them a chance to feel good about themselves. Bringing out their best stuff pulls them into positive cycles.

A massive body of data gathered by Gallup proves that our strengths deserve far more time than our shortcomings. But the prevailing opinion, worldwide, is that success depends mainly on overcoming our weaknesses instead of developing and exploiting our unique gifts. Researcher Tom Rath states,

"In every culture we have studied, the overwhelming majority of parents (77 percent in the U.S.) think that a student's lowest grades deserve the most time and attention. Parents and teachers reward excellence with apathy instead of investing more time in the areas where a child has the most potential for greatness."[20]

The same pattern shows up in the way we run organizations and manage our personal lives. Gallup data on 10 million people reveal that 7 million don't have the opportunity to focus on what they do best in the work environment. This carries tremendous cost and brings negativity into our everyday lives. In *StrengthsFinder 2.0*, Rath reports that if you're not playing in your sweet spot, chances are you—

- **Dread going to work**

- **Have more negative than positive interactions with colleagues**

- **Treat customers poorly**

- **Tell friends you work for a miserable outfit**

- **Achieve less on a daily basis**

- **Have fewer positive and creative moments**[21]

Operating outside the sweet spots of our unique gifts also works against our health and relationships with others.

Surprisingly, neutral behavior (for example, having a boss who ignores you) is even more detrimental than working for someone who focuses on your weaknesses. If your manager ignores you, the chances of your being actively disengaged on the job are 40 percent. This compares with only a 22 percent rate of disengagement when the boss focuses on weaknesses, and a mere 1 percent rate when the focus is on strengths.[22]

People who get to use their unique gifts every day are six times as likely to be engaged in their work. They're also three times as likely to report having an excellent quality of life in general.[23]

Put yourself in a positive frame of mind by playing to your sweet spot. Then pull others into positive cycles by helping them engage their unique gifts.

If we can hit that bull's-eye,
the rest of the dominoes will fall like
a house of cards ... Checkmate.

— ZAPP BRANNIGAN

Epilogue

The Knowledge Economy ushered in a new era of leadership because it changed the very nature of work, but most people have failed to make corresponding adjustments in the way they attempt to lead. They're ignoring the cognitive factors that now contribute most to high performance.

Top executives know intuitively that deep strengths carry tremendous influence over an organization's ability to perform. That's a good sign, but it's time to actually do something with that knowledge.

In fact, leaders have a fiduciary responsibility to protect and nurture their organization's deep strengths, because this represents part of a company's net worth. Deep strengths are simply a different class of assets— intangible and ephemeral like a brand, but perhaps with more inherent value than an organization's hard assets. It's worth noting that, at the beginning of the twenty-first century, Coca-Cola had an estimated brand value of over $72 billion. How much might deep strengths be worth?

STILL WATERS RUN DEEP

Organizations spend big and strategize at length to build their brands, yet hardly a dollar gets invested in developing deep strengths. Does this make any sense at all?

We know that performance begins inside the head, that it is born of our thoughts and emotions. We also know that this "inner game" is influenced to a great degree by the behavior cycles we engage in with other people. The person-to-person loops that fill our small moments continually shape us as human beings, leaving us either more or less effective than we were the day before.

If you're trying to gain competitive advantage, you should concentrate on muscling up the corporate psyche, because this is the hidden realm where results originate. Devote top management attention, and budget, to building these invisible assets.

BACK TO THE FUTURE

Strength training is important because, as the saying goes, "The weak get hit by sickness first." I would add, "The strong get their turn at the food bowl first." And that, of course, contributes to their getting stronger still.

As the past can tell us, tomorrow will surely take us by surprise, offering up astonishing opportunities while also blindsiding us with unexpected changes. The best way to prepare for this future is to develop our deep strengths.

Enough, Friend.
If you want to read on, Then go, yourself
become the book and its essence.

— ANGELUS SILESIUS

RESOURCES

1. C. Snyder, C. Wiklund, and J. Cheavens, "Hope and Success in College," a paper presented at the annual meeting of the American Psychological Association (Boston, August 1999).

2. Teresa M. Amabile and Steven J. Kramer, "Inner Work Life: Understanding the Subtext of Business Performance," *Harvard Business Review*, Vol. 85, No. 5 (May, 2007): 80.

3. Paul G. Stoltz, *Adversity Quotient* (New York: John Wiley & Sons, 1997), 68.

4. Holly J. Morris, "Happiness Explained: New Science Shows How to Inject Real Joy into Your Life," *U.S. News & World Report* (September 3, 2001): 46–55.

5. Sara Schaefer Munoz, "Cost to Treat a Depression Case Falls; Bigger Share of Sufferers Are Now Receiving Help, So Total Expenditures Rise," *The Wall Street Journal,* Eastern edition (December 31, 2003), D2.

6. Steve Crabtree, "Getting Personal in the Workplace: Are Negative Relationships Squelching Productivity in Your Company?" *Gallup Management Journal* (June 10, 2004). Retrieved February 23, 2005, from http://gmj.gallup.com/print/?ci=11956.

7. Tom Rath and Donald O. Clifton, *How Full Is Your Bucket?* (New York: Gallup Press, 2004), 47.

8. John Gottman, *Why Marriages Succeed or Fail...and How You Can Make Yours Last* (New York: Fireside, 1994), 57.

9. Daniel Goleman, *Social Intelligence* (New York: Bantam Dell, 2006), 18.

10. Daniel H. Pink, *A Whole New Mind* (New York: Riverhead Books, 2005), 156.

11. Malcolm Gladwell, *Blink* (New York: Little, Brown and Company, 2005), 208.

12. Robert Rosenthal and Lenore Jacobson, *Pygmalion in the Classroom: Teacher Expectation and Pupils' Intellectual Development* (Carmathen, United Kingdom: Crown House Publishing, 2003), 61-97.

13. Robert Rosenthal and K. L. Fode, "The Effect of Experimenter Bias on the Performance of the Albino Rat," *Behaviorial Science*, 8 (1963): 183-189.

14. H. Yuan, D. Clifton, P. Stone, and H. Blumberg, "Positive and Negative Words: Their Association with Leadership Talent and Effectiveness," *The Psychologist-Manager Journal,* Vol. 2, No. 2 (2000): 199.

15. Tom Rath, "The Best Ways to Recognize Employees," *Gallup Management Journal* (December 9, 2004). Retrieved February 23, 2005, from http://gmj.gallup.com/print/?ci=13888.

16. Daniel Goleman, Richard Boyatzis, and Annie McKee, *Primal Leadership* (Boston: Harvard Business School Press, 2002), 10.

17. Fabio Sala, "Laughing All the Way to the Bank," *Harvard Business Review*, Vol. 81, No. 10 (September 2003): 16–17.

18. Daniel Goleman, Richard Boyatzis, and Annie McKee, *Primal Leadership*, 34.

19. Daniel H. Pink, *A Whole New Mind*, 58.

20. Tom Rath, *StrengthsFinder 2.0* (New York: Gallup Press, 2007), 7.

21. Ibid, 12.

22. Ibid, iv.

23. Ibid, iii.

ABOUT THE AUTHOR

Price Pritchett, Ph.D., is Chairman and CEO of PRITCHETT, LP, a Dallas-based consulting, training, and publishing firm with offices in eight countries. He has spent 30 years advising top management and boards of directors of major corporations, governmental organizations, and not-for-profits, with his work taking him to Europe, Asia, and throughout the Americas.

Pritchett's thought leadership in merger integration, organizational change, and corporate culture has been referenced in most of the major business journals and newspapers. He also has been interviewed on CNN, CNBC, and other major television channels. With over 20 million copies of his books in print world-wide, he is one of the best-selling business authors in the world. Virtually all of the *Fortune* 500 companies have used some combination of PRITCHETT's consulting, training, and publications.